Acknowledgements

I thank Almighty God for inspiring me to write this book for children across America and the world about the absence of fathers or father figures in the home. It is my hope and prayer that this book will encourage mothers and resident fathers to remain steadfast in their daily struggle to raise the banner of love and harmony. In order for our children who are the future to lead a productive life, parents must set an example. The pages of this book are written to touch the hearts and minds of those fathers who have neglected their responsibility. Hopefully, it will also help them find once again their irreplaceable position in the life of their child and thus begin the healing process in the child's broken spirit.

It is a joy to have friends and family who believe in me and willingly gave of themselves to make my dream a reality. Special thanks are extended to Gwendolyn Fowlkes and Beverly Garvin for editing. Dr. Janet Mays, Joyce Battle, Attorney Victor Douglas and Dr. Elmorie Miller are commended for providing their perceptions on interacting with children who do not have fathers in their homes. Additionally they rendered valuable advice on how the School System may assist children with absentee fathers become productive members of society. I am grateful to my daughter who encouraged me to write this book. I humbly thank and praise my wondrously talented illustrators, Cheryl Tarnoski and Tony Brown for their artistic expressions.

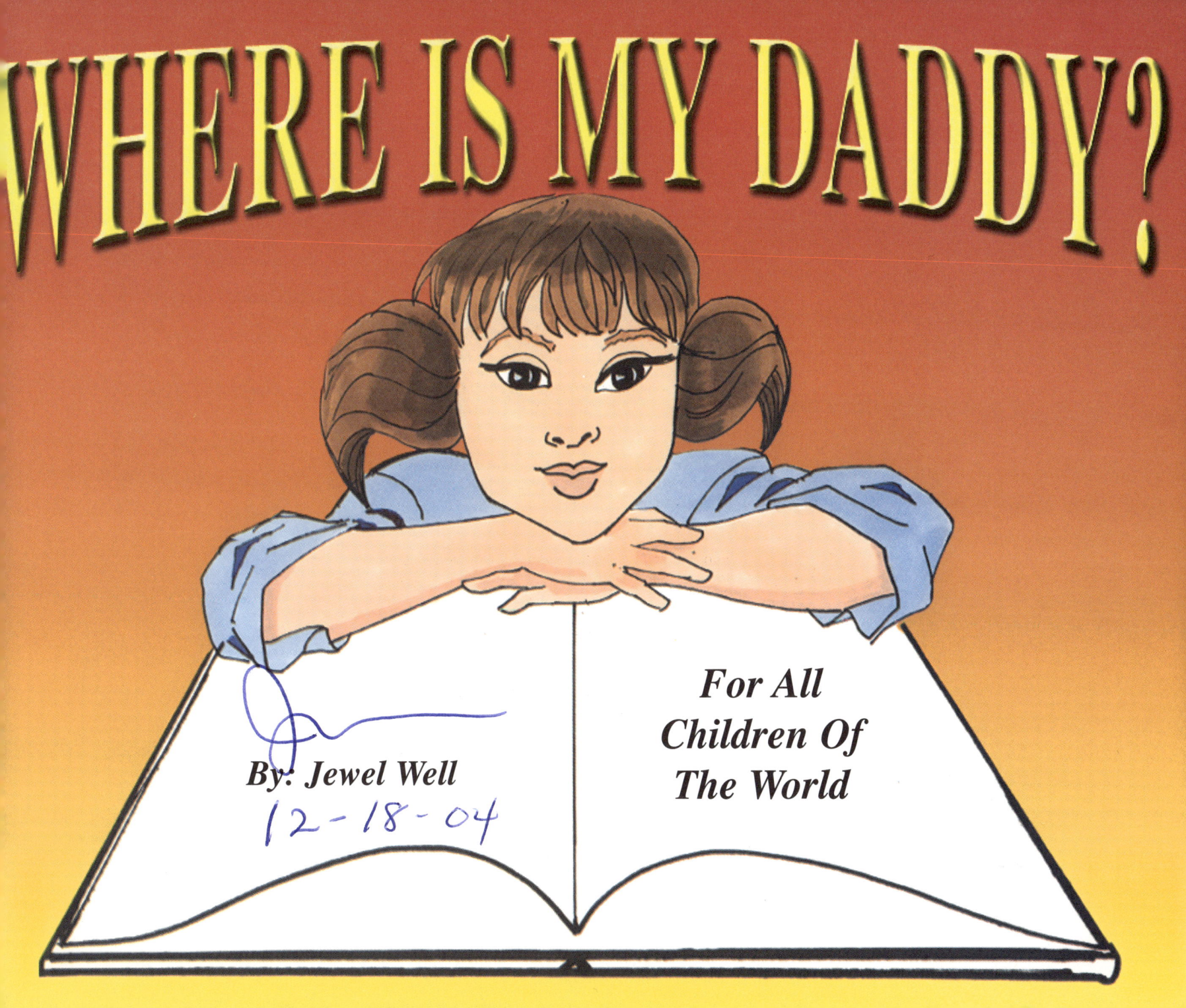

Published by Jewel Well

Illustrations Tony Brown and Cheryl Tarnoski

Design and Printed by **MAYS PRINTING CO., INC**
Detroit, Michigan, U.S.A. • (313) 861-1900 • A Certified Minority Printer

All rights reserved. No part of this publication may be reproduced, stored in a retrieval system, or transmitted in any form or by means, electronic, mechanical, photocopying, recording or otherwise, without the prior permission of the publisher.

Permission to reproduce any part of this story or illustration must be obtained in writing from Jewel Well at P.O. Box 312116, Detroit, Michigan 48231-2116

First Edition

Library of Congress Catalog Card Number: TXu1-163-855
ISBN: 09743601

Table of Contents

Introduction 1

A Prayer for Missing Fathers 3

Chapter 1   Daddy. 7

Chapter 2   Symptoms of Behavior. 23

Chapter 3   Parenting 31

Chapter 4   From Destructive to Productive Behavior 39

Chapter 5   Teenagers Ashley and Charlie Chat — Go Deep, Real Deep.........................45
                         (Parental Discretion Recommended)

Introduction

This book aims to identify the social, physical and emotional behavior of those children with absentee fathers, including those who have no suitable alternative or support system to aid in their healthy, balanced development. It may also serve to enable children to overcome their challenges and become self-fulfilled and competitive in school and other meaningful areas of society.

A Prayer for Missing Fathers

Dear Father,

Hear us, we pray, Heavenly Father, as with burning hearts we sit staring out our windows waiting for our fathers to come. Most of the time, God, we cry late at night in our beds. Please do not let our tears be silent. We are brokenhearted but we still love our fathers anyway.

Hear us, Lord, in these words we say to our missing fathers: "We love you wherever you are. Only you can give us the hugs and kisses we hunger for so much inside."

Dear God, please stop our fathers from letting us down when they never return our calls or never send us a letter expressing how they feel about us. Lord, tell our fathers we do not want to hear anymore excuses why he cannot spend time with his child.

Dear Lord, does he love us - when a knock on the door is never heard from our fathers? Was he too busy for us? Sometimes, Lord, we just want to take the wings of a bird and fly far away, never to be heard again. Oh, how it hurts inside of us, not knowing if our fathers really care about us. The tears we shed reflect our brokenhearts. We ask you, God, why do our fathers rip our hearts apart so much? The pain and agony inside of us taunts us daily, wondering where he is.

Heavenly Father, we call on your name. Please help us to restore our dreams that do not come true. Let us see our father's faces. Let us hear our father's voices, please dear God, before the day becomes night. We do not need to hear "See you later" from them anymore. We want our missing fathers in our lives. Dear God, only you can reach our fathers now.

Thank you God. We love you for hearing our prayer. Amen.

"Look Annie, look Pepper! That big star there must be the Daddy in the great big family of stars!"

chapter one

DADDY!

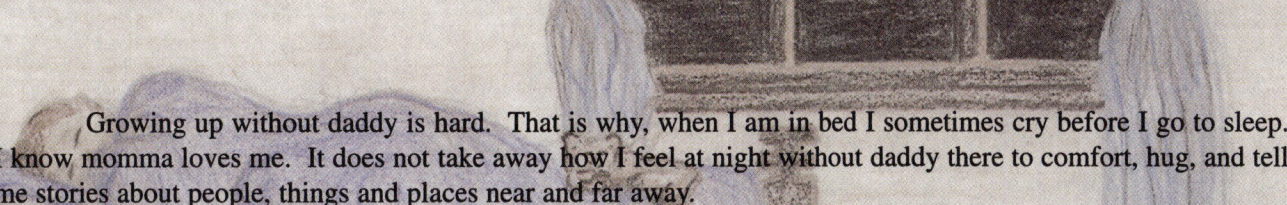

Growing up without daddy is hard. That is why, when I am in bed I sometimes cry before I go to sleep. I know momma loves me. It does not take away how I feel at night without daddy there to comfort, hug, and tell me stories about people, things and places near and far away.

I try hard not to cry and show my feelings. Sometimes I cannot help it. Then momma gets that far away look on her face all over again. When she thinks I am sleeping, she begins to stare out the window. She does not know I am looking at her when she thinks I am asleep. I see her blowing in her handkerchief, wiping her running nose and face as she stares out my bedroom window. I wonder what she is thinking as she looks real hard up toward the sky. Maybe it is about the day I came into the world and what she was doing . . . or maybe even before, of a special moment of fun which she misses or something.

This is how it makes me feel inside:

DADDY! DADDY!
Tear drops of pain running down
My sad face.
Wanting you, DADDY, to be close beside me,
To see this world.
As I call you, DADDY! DADDY!

From the cradle,
To my youth, the voice I want to hear
Across my bed,
Is Daddy, whispering "I love you".
Gently take my hand.
Hold me tightly, so I will not be scared.

I can see animals licking the fur on their offspring, and scaring away any animals who seem to get too close. What's up with that, Dad? Did you forget Momma and me?

I know who my daddy is, but he never comes to see me. What kind of daddy is it who could create me with my momma, a child of his own flesh, blood, mind, heart and sweat only to forget about me? Momma tells me I look just like him and if I want to see him to just look in the mirror. I wonder if he sees me when he looks into his mirror? Does he miss me? Does he know me, think about me? Does he care? I think about it often.

Sometimes I even imagine my daddy being a test tube in one of those laboratories I see in the movies. He may as well be, it seems. Or maybe Mother Nature blew me in through the window from some place outside and dropped me off at this address.

I have questions.

Even animals have families. I have seen it myself, either outside or at the zoo. Are not human animals too? Do we eat, sleep, work and play as the animals do?

Daddy, I want answers to these and many, many more questions. Where are you? I want to play Nintendo, go horseback riding on you, enjoy Playstation and walk in your big, big shoes. Gimmie some money. Better yet, gimmie some love, Daddy!

This poem is about animals nurturing their offspring.

DADDY, DADDY!
DO I BELONG TO YOU, DADDY?
I SEE THE BIRD WITH ITS OFFSPRING.
I SEE THE BEAR WITH ITS OFFSPRING.
I SEE THE LION WITH ITS OFFSPRING.
I SEE THE KANGAROO WITH ITS OFFSPRING.
BUT DADDY!
I DO NOT SEE YOU WITH YOUR OFFSPRING.

Where is he?
Hope he is out there.

Daddy! The other day my best friend, Marsha, brought her daddy to the school play to see her perform the lead role of Cinderella. I was in it also. I played her supporting actor, the fairy godmother. When it was over, her daddy gave her a great big hug. I did not know where you were. I had not seen you since that time momma saw you at the corner store. (Before that we bumped into you accidentally at the festival when you were with that lady, last year). After the play, I hid backstage so Marsha could not see me cry. At that very moment I wished I was Marsha. I do not talk with her anymore. I hate Marsha. Also, I hate that I hate Marsha. I love you! Come home daddy, so that I do not have to hate Marsha or anybody, anymore.

Daddy, I used to cry myself to sleep with Pepper, my dog, and Annie, my doll, because they were the only things close to me that I could call my own. Many days we would sit on the porch waiting and hoping you would show up to see me. My heart would be so full of tears that I would long for you to be around me.

I used to stare out the window hoping you would come by. Pepper would bark and I would imagine it might be you knocking at the front door to take us to buy ice cream or a slush. I hated sitting down to eat breakfast and dinner without you. Lots of times I would stop eating to run to my room and lay across my bed with tears in my eyes, thinking of you. I always imagined how it would be to have both parents in the home.

How does it feel, daddy, knowing you have missed a lot of my birthday parties and important events in my life? When I was in the third grade, I was nominated by my school to compete against other students from other schools for the State spelling bee contest. I invited you to attend and you never responded. I even waited before I went out on the stage and looked into the audience once again to see if you were there. I was so hurt and angry that I misspelled the word 'catastrophe' on purpose because that is how I felt my life was.

I ran track in the sixth grade just to let out my frustrations because I felt I was not totally and completely loved by you, daddy. When I ran the 100 yard dash, I ran as though the fire that burned on the inside of me was being put out. The people in the bleachers chanted and shouted my name. The wind would beat around my back and my eyes would be full of tears. The sweat from my back released every pain that was hurting me deep down in my soul. At the end of the track when I crossed the finish line, I looked back. Only then did I realize the other kids were not even close to keeping up with me.

Everyone applauded my singing, but Daddy never came. "You love me! You really love me!"

Sometimes I would become real angry because I did not have a real daddy to play baseball or share in sports events. Just to have seen his face would have made all the difference in the world. With my daddy, it would have made my life happier so I would not be tempted to throw temper tantrums at other kids who had daddies. I would sit on the porch with my catcher's mitt on and throw the ball over and over, back and forth in my mitt. My grandmother would become unhappy because she knew that I would be thinking about not having a daddy to play with. Walking down my street, I would see other daddies playing with their kids. Tears would fill my eyes. I would find a tree to sit under where I could cry to myself. Oh, how I wish I had a daddy to play with me! At times I could even hear my older sister crying in her room for the two of us.

There is one event in my life that I will never forget, you did not show up. It was my eighth grade graduation and I had sent you an invitation. I was so mad and hurt that day because you were not there for me. I wanted to make you very proud of me, the smartest eighth grade student who received achievement awards for science fair, debate team, honor roll and gymnastics, and you were not there. I had taken several pictures with everyone except you, daddy, before the graduation started. I wanted you there so I could tell my friends, "Here is my daddy". That did not happen.

I called you several times that day. I left you several messages telling you what I would be wearing at my graduation. I truly wanted you to attend. When I walked across the stage to receive my certificate, I glanced through the entire audience several times and noticed that you were not there. My mom told me later that you were at a business meeting and could not attend. That day I became sick to my stomach before the ceremony was over. I rushed right into the bathroom after receiving my certificate. I did not want to embarrass myself in front of my friends after the graduation. I had already bragged to them the night before that my daddy was attending and how handsome he was. So I stayed in the bathroom until my mom came and found me.

When I got home I sat down in the kitchen and cried my heart out to God. "God, why did you allow me to have a father who does not love me or see all the good things I do with my life?" I will always remember that day because you were not there for me. Oftentimes I have replayed this event back and forth in my mind. "Why, Why did you not attend my eighth grade graduation?" I felt that a child support check could never replace spending time with your child.

During my dance recital, I danced as if there was no tomorrow. When I saw my friends with their fathers praising them for their dance routines, I became so sad. You should have been standing in the audience applauding and praising the efforts of your daughter. It was just another let down from my daddy. I wrote a poem about how children feel:

We as children are crying.
We need guidance and direction.
Help us now! Do Not Wait!
Sing to us a lullaby.

We need to believe in ourselves.
Teach us how to pray.
So when we call out God's name
He will hear us clearly.

If we seek out the Master Parent,
God will send a stream of knowledge to flow
Like a river within us. We will be taught
To love all of God's children.

Children are planted as fruit in their parents.
They are God's gift to parents.
When parents teach and nurture their babies
Sparkling and glorious jewels are formed.

God teaches us to love each other.
Single parents must love in spite of rejection.
In this kind of harmony, only loved
And wanted children are created.

Children want boys to become men and
Girls to become women before they become parents.
Then together they can take care of their children.
So we will not have to long for missing daddies.

The Greatest Moment

In My Life

The Greatest Moment In My Life

The greatest moment in my life occurred when I was nine years old. I played the piano and sang a song at a talent show. I was well received by a captivated audience who applauded me. They made me feel special. No one had ever made me feel that way before except my mother. Thinking back on my music, I would be sitting down sometimes and a song would be ringing in my ear. My music and songs would make the pain of missing my daddy go away. One of my little songs went like this:

I sing a song of love.
I sing a song to everyone.
Because the world needs love
Come and join this love.

I hope it touches your heart.
Many people do not know how to love.
I sing this to them.
In the hope that it reaches their heart.

Many children need that love.
So I sing a song of love.
And hope it reaches their heart.
What we need today is love.
Is l-o-v-e la la la la.

I wonder what the moment would have been like if it had been you, Dad, instead of Ronald?

When the children on my block would come outside to play, I would suck my thumb for security from the pain inside of me. They would tease me. Then I would ride my bike up and down the street daydreaming that you were riding beside me. I painted so many pictures in my mind of what my real father would do with me. Then I would go into my room and be sad all over again. Finally, I would draw a happy picture because I knew my mother loved me, and tried so very hard to make up for the parenting that you as a father should have been giving me.

I fantasized a lot. These fantasies allowed me to escape my fears of not having a father. I painted pictures of how it would be to have a real father. If my daddy would have just said a few words to me, that would have meant so much to me. I would like to share this poem with others like myself:

> Do not let me fantasize.
> Let me see reality.
> Do not let me hide, help me.
> I want to see the real you.
> Daddy! I am hurting.
> Where is the picture of you
> I painted in my mind?

My mother says I act just like you; although, you do not live with us, a part of you still lives inside of me. My mother smiles when I mention my father's name. Sometimes when she sees me doing things, she says, "You act just like your father." Is it in my genes to be like my father? Of course I have your genes living inside of me since you are my father! This poem is "I want to be me."

> I see you,
> I see me,
> I feel you,
> Inside of me.

Daddy why could I not spend the night with you? Many nights I dreamed that Pepper, Annie and I came over to spend the night with you. You made so many broken promises to me about spending the night. I often thought you just did not want me around. Many days I felt sad and lonely after being let down. This poem tells you how I feel about you:

DADDY! DADDY!
I was never invited.
DADDY! DADDY!
I was shut out.
DADDY! DADDY!
Why didn't you?
DADDY! DADDY!
Let me in.

* * * * * *

DADDY,
That which lives inside me is love.
That love burns daily in my heart.
You have not helped me to become
Ashley, the total me.

I am filled with light around me
That will not go out.
You were not in my life,
To teach me how to love.
My life will go on.

chapter two

Symptoms of Behavior

PART I : The Child's Symptoms of Pain

1. Rage
2. Anger
3. Hurt
4. Distress

    Ashley is in a rage because her father did not return her phone calls. She is angry. She thinks her father does not care about her. She feels lonely and hurt. Ashley blames her mother for getting involved with her father in the first place. Most of the time she is angry because her mother does not listen to her.

5. Panting
6. Screaming
7. Crying
8. Cursing

    At times, Charlie wants to stop breathing because he sees his friends interacting with their fathers in the home. He sees his friends playing with and being hugged by their fathers. He sees fathers showing genuine affection for their children. Charlie is frustrated because his father has abandoned him. He wants to scream and use profanity out of frustration. He cries himself to sleep and wishes that he had never been born.

9. Moody
10. Undecided
11. Disturbed
12. Withdrawn
13. Stubborn

Ashley holds her feelings inside while she is around others. She has developed low self-esteem. When asked a question, Ashley can never give you a straight answer. She often says, "I am not sure" or "I do not care". She is quick to withdraw from others. She has an uncooperative attitude. Her favorite phrase is, "Quit bothering me". Often she tells her mother to close the door to her bedroom. Ashley throws temper tantrums without knowing she has demonstrated displaced anger. Ashley feels she is not complete without her father in the home.

Charlie has a lot of anger inside. His vocabulary is vulgar and profane and he uses these words with teachers, students and friends. Charlie identifies with being tough. His mother is in and out of drug rehabilitation. Home life is dismal. Charlie sleeps on a cold floor and hardly has any clothes to wear. The home is almost bare of furniture except for a worn out television. The neighborhood is in shambles. Someone in the neighborhood is getting shot today. Charlie blames God for allowing him to be born in hell. Listen to his pain:

Siren sounding
Someone crying.
Someone running.
Someone screaming.
Someone saying,
"Oh, Oh! Another junkie
Just checked out for life".

14. Distrust
15. Daydreaming
16. Defensive
17. Irate

Ashley has difficulty trusting others because her father abandoned her. Ashley relies on her mother to be totally supportive and honest with her. As Ashley attempts to overcome her feelings of inadequacy and low self-esteem, she needs to know that her mother will always be in her corner. She often stares at others and daydreams, comparing their life to her own. Ashley is always on the defensive and ready to challenge anyone who questions what she is trying to say. Ashley can become very irate in the classroom when she fails to get everyone's attention quickly.

Charlie's mother has lied to him repeatedly. She has stated on numerous occasions that she would stop doing drugs and promised that they would do things together. As a result, Charlie does not trust anyone. Charlie's foremost thought is survival. He steals from other students and teachers just to have food to eat. Charlie is violent and obscene with everyone.

Part II: The Child's Defense

1. The Red Eye

The red eye is the most visibly expressed behavior. It is a type of behavior exemplified by constant fighting, red eyes, and irrational anger. It indicates that the child is out of control and does not like himself or others. The child has nothing good to say about anyone. The pent up anger is explosive.

2. Close The Bedroom Door

This allows the child to fantasize and create the worst possible scenario about himself. It is called the "Beat MYSELF Syndrome." This is a sign of depression. When the child is left alone the usual activity is to watch television, listen to the radio, or chat on the Internet. The television and radio destroy the positive imagination of a child. This media also provides negative role models for the child. The Internet may unleash unwanted 'friends' who prey on children while their parents are too busy to notice.

3. Children's Tales

Mothers never listen. Mothers do not cook the food children like. Mothers and children cannot talk because their perceptions are different. Children can talk to their friends but not to their mothers. Mothers never understand explanations for being out past curfew. For example: "The car had a flat" or "I was over my friend's house" or "I thought you said be home at 12:00 a.m." Often single mothers are not home enough to tell children what to do. Therefore, children must become independent and make their own adult like decisions. Children think they are adults.

4. On the Edge

Children feel stressed out when parents are making simple requests such as 'take out the garbage, wash dishes, clean your room' or any other chore. They invent excuses for not performing chores or finishing their homework. Children tend to resent and blame the teacher if they receive poor grades. Bringing home failing grades causes more tension and stress for the child. To obtain relief from the pressures at home, the child seeks out friends and peers. Children escape from the reality of home life by experimenting with drugs, alcohol and sex.

5. The Father's Genes

A portion of a child's behavior is due to hereditary factors. When a mother keeps telling the child that they remind her of their biological father, the child seizes the opportunity to act out. This can serve a dual purpose. One is an affirmation that "Dad" is real. The other is frustration over the fact that mom is the only parent present.

6. Classroom Behavior

The child takes on annoying and disruptive behavior that prevents others from learning. This behavior may take the form of throwing spitballs and paper airplanes, fighting in the classroom, using profanity, refusing to understand or perform the work, and talking loudly while instructions are being given. The teacher must be able to identify the student's negative behavior and resolve the problem before further interruption of the learning process occurs. This behavior impedes the learning of others.

Part III: The Child's Reactions to Others

Ashley begins to act like her father who is not living in the home. Her behavior has changed. Ashley disrespects her mother and friends by making unreasonable demands in lieu of simply asking. She constantly snaps at others and interrupts their conversation. Her tone of voice is loud and obnoxious. She is never giving, but always taking. Whenever things do not go her way, she becomes mean spirited.

Charlie disrespects everyone because he thinks no one cares about him. The only time Charlie feels good is when he is fighting someone in the classroom. Only then can the teacher instruct Charlie because school is the only place where Charlie can release his frustrations and anxieties. Charlie displays an attitude because he is angry. He does not have a father or nurturing mother.

Ashley gets upset when her friends do not take care of business when going places. For example, Ashley becomes irate if concert tickets are not picked up when requested. She constantly thinks of self. Ashley blames others for her irrational behavior. She might say, "Oh, my friends think only of themselves. That is why I did not go where I wanted to go."

Charlie becomes depressed because everything he attempts to manipulate and scheme falls apart. Whenever he is sent to the office for disruptive behavior, the counselor questions his farfetched explanations instead of accepting them as fact. The least little thing upsets him. Charlie becomes annoyed because others are not speaking in his profane dialect and will not listen to him. Charlie daydreams about being a world renown rapper. When Charlie is immersed in the fantasy world, he is fine. Once he is forced out of his illusions he becomes moody and hard to get along with and is ready to fight because his real world is a nightmare.

chapter three

Parenting

The television and radio present a society where few children reach 18 years of age with a natural father in the home. United States statistics indicate that 50% of children are without fathers in the home before the age of 18. One reason is that too many young people are having children before they reach 21 years of age. How does one who has never really experienced being reared by a mother and father raise a child when they themselves lack parenting skills?

Too often there is no family relationship between the child's parents. They are not married. Further, even when a child is born into a marriage, custody of the child usually goes to the mother if a break up occurs.

Children today lack guidance. There is no one in the home to help unless their mother has older children. New mothers today feel they only have time for their own children. Other parents will see a child deviate from normal behavior and will not care or inform the child's parents. They will often say, "That is not my child and I have my own to worry about." Many times neighbors will be at home looking out their window and viewing everything a child is doing. They will not inform the parent. They will help another mother only if it involves their child. What ever happened to parents helping others in the neighborhood? Car pooling is not enough, especially when there are a large number of single parents joining the work force.

The continuity of any community lies in the health and welfare of its children. Getting involved with neighbors makes a more cohesive community possible. When children know that others care, their behavior is better.

The father may leave the familial relationship when there are constant arguments with the mother. Then the father spends less and less time with the child. When the child is alone, he or she becomes depressed and begins to blame himself or herself for the parental breakup. In school the child may exhibit behavioral changes because he or she is angry that the biological father is gone. The child's behavior may become rebellious or withdrawn.

Ashley grew up without a father. She tried to communicate with him daily through letters, telephone calls and email. He rejected Ashley. Ashley began having psychological problems by the time she reached the age of eight. Others like Ashley develop low self-worth. They feel worthless at times. For example, at times they feel like, "I cannot do anything right". Ashley ran across her father in a department store. He ran over to her and said, "Hello". He attempted to strike up a conversation with Ashley. She did not want to hear what he had to say. Ashley had only seen her father briefly on holidays. When he finally realized Ashley was not going to communicate with him, he said, "Your mother turned you against me."

Ashley replied, "You did it all by yourself. I waited for you many days and you never came. I would call you most of the time all day and night. You did not respond. Who is to blame? From the time I became a teenager, we have lived in the same city. Did you ever bother to pick me up from school? You even put your answering machine on when I called to explain that I did not have a ride to school. When I needed a car because my mother had to work, you said, "It is your mother's problem." Finally, you said you would let me drive your car and you never did. Where have you been? So called daddy, stay out of my life."

Many mothers become angry and resentful when the child exemplifies traits of the absentee father. The manifestation of the father's gene in the child's character has caused many mothers to shake their heads in pain and disbelief. Everything the mother has taught the child seems to fly out of the window. The child is determined to behave like their biological father. Mothers often try to put blinders on, deceiving themselves into thinking the child could not be like the biological father.

The mother should listen and immediately provide solutions that will correct the child's behavior. Labeling the child as 'stupid', 'dumb' or 'just like your father' serves to deflate the child's self-esteem. Mothers need to zero in on the problem and deal with the child's behavior instead of resorting to "name calling". Possible solutions are:

1. Make a note of the child's behavior or capture it on video.

2. The mother should sit down with the child and calmly listen to their justifications for various patterns of behavior. The mother should be careful not to display disapproval with her body language or constant interruptions and questions.

3. It is essential that the mother pay close attention and maintain eye contact with the child. She should not be talking on the telephone, talking to the other children, entertaining boyfriends, watching television, or otherwise distracted.

4. Once both the child and the mother identify the problem, corrective actions should be used to resolve the problem.

5. If the child has created the problem, take away television, telephone, cell phone and automobile. Remove other privileges such as going to the movies, the computer and play time with pets and friends. Make sure the child's bedroom door remains open unless the child is getting dressed or undressed.

6. The child's new activities would be to read a short story each week and go to the library. Make the child more responsible by providing them with chores such as vacumming, sweeping the kitchen floor, washing dishes, doing laundry, cleaning their room and finally, learning how to cook.

7. Mothers need to play a more active role in Parent Teacher Conferences. Attend PTA meetings. Assist the child with his/her homework. Request weekly progress reports from teachers. Mothers may pay an impromptu visit to the child's school to observe classroom behavior. If necessary, the mother may need to sit in the classroom with the child to observe the child's behavior in the classroom with the teacher's permission. The mother may need to take a leave of absence from work to ensure the stability of the child.

8. Mothers should go to the park or take a walk with the child. It would be helpful for mothers to participate in a sports activity or hobby with the child. The parent and child could get involved in community programs. The goal of these activities is to establish a loving and trusting relationship between mother and child. Community programs could be available through a local church. Mother-Daughter support groups are just one of the excellent programs provided by churches.

9. The mother should give examples and demonstrate good and bad behavior to the child. Most importantly, take time to listen to the child. This may be the key to a turning point for the child. Hold the child in your arms. Hug the child. From the heart say to the child, "I love you".

10. Mothers who need help as well as the child should obtain counseling. If mothers are on drugs or alcohol they should seek a rehabilitation program. Mothers who provide their children with negative feedback should replace the name calling and labeling with positive reinforcements.

   A few examples are:

   - Do not call your children "B..." which is a female dog. Please call them by their birth name.
   - This slang language "Yeah! Dog" and "What's up Dog" need to be replaced with a slang "What's up." We must introduce to our children a better way of communication.
   - You are a Great Woman or You are a Great Man.
   - God made you a total being with substance.
   - God will give you a greater vision of success if you seek Him.
   - I know I can count on you.
   - I know you can do it.
   - Let's do it together!
   - We are a family.
   - I love you because you are special.

11. The mother still has a responsibility to nurture a healthy child. When the child is put out of the home for various reasons, the mother still can monitor the situation from a distance. Mother should not at any time abandon their responsibility as a parent. The child already has been abandoned by their father and does not need further abandonment.

    - Mothers can initiate ministers and relatives for support.
    - A daily dialog regardless whose right or wrong. There must be a resolution by both to reach the child. Do not leave your responsibility up to the world to resolve your problem. Remember your child is not an adult or thinks like an adult. Putting a child out might be your only choice but you should monitor the child's whereabouts to make sure they are safe. Children need to be loved by their parents first.
    - As a parent, you must communicate with your child's friends mother while the child is temporarily living in their home. Do not leave the responsibility up to your friend's mother to raise your child.
    - If you cannot support your child, then seek help. Call a nearby church group or organization for counseling. Remember there are people out there that are willing to help you.
    - Help your teenager find employment. Do not put them out and say I can no longer support you. The child depends on you as a parent.
    - The mother must set an example with their children. Allowing your child to suffer because you are in an unstable relationship is no excuse as a mother.
    - Complete abandonment is no excuse. Seek God and pray. God will give you the answers to raise your child. Sometimes, prayer is not enough it must be accompanied by fasting and one must be led how to fast.

BE YE ANGRY AND SIN NOT:
let not the sun go down upon your wrath:
Ephesians 4:26

And ye fathers, provoke not your child to wrath:
but bring them up in the nurture
and admonition of Lord.
Ephesians 6:4

. . .And this one is for Dad!

*I have never been happy.
Never, never, never,
have I been happy.*

Never, Never, Never, Never, Never, Never, Never, Never, Never, Never, Never, Never, Never, Never, Nev

chapter four

From Destructive To Productive Behavior

Ignoring problems will not make them disappear. The result is anxiety, depression, and other major problems. Often when a child suppresses his feelings they explode through fighting, profanity and disruptive behavior in the classroom. The child needs to overcome his behavior by discussing the anxiety with mothers, friends, teachers, counselors and close relatives. Silent behavior may lead to destruction. The child must let go of the past of (having been abandoned by his father). The child must make the following decisions:

1. I will overcome my feelings of frustration and anger.
2. I will stop blaming myself for not having a father in the home.
3. I can still be happy even though my biological father abandoned me.
4. I must not allow myself to become a victim of my past by replaying over and over in my head what he did not do. I must reprogram my mind.
5. Forgiving my father will be a step-by-step process.
6. When I am angry, I will breathe in and out several times to release my unhappiness.
7. I will stop being jealous of my friends who have a father in the home.
8. I accept that we are not in a perfect world.
9. I will focus on positive activities. For example, I can improve my situation by getting a job; performing community service and joining after school programs.
10. I will become more responsible with my time.

SPELLING BEE

C... A... T... A... S... T... R... A... F... R... Y

Of course they would give Ashley the one word she never would admit knowing all too well! (She could have spelled it backward even if she wanted to!)

Numerous successful male mentoring programs have been set up. There is a great need to enlarge these programs. Creating new ones is also paramount. Today this type of program is needed at all levels including elementary school.

Part of a successful reconciliation between a child and its father is the ability for the child to have freedom of expression. To express feelings of hurt and abandonment, the child could write down what he feels and why. This should be accomplished prior to discussing these feelings with the father. The child and father may start communicating through email, letters and telephone calls. Once the child and father start talking, it is essential to keep the lines of communication open. Building up the relationship between father and child may start with five to ten minute conversations. Then communications may be held during 30 minute meetings, phone calls, Internet chats. Once frequent and meaningful conversations are implemented the child may then start feeling comfortable around the father again. On the other hand, if the child does not know his father he may communicate his feelings to close relatives and friends.

Darwin's theory of male dominance may be the reason why some kids join gangs. According to that theory, the child joins gangs in order to gain acceptance and approval. If, therefore, the child considers joining for this reason he must ask himself prior to joining, "Will this make me happy?" or, "Am I seeking the love and protection I am not getting at home?" "If I choose this type of gang, will I wind up dead eventually?" Your best friend might not be able to answer these questions. It is suggested that the child consult with his parent, teacher or counselor.

The behavior of parents is a critical factor in determining the outcome of their children's lives. Parents should be leaders and role models guiding the child. They should serve as positive reinforcers of desired behaviors along with cultivating the mind of the child. Spending quality time with a child is invaluable. It is one of the clearest expressions of love that can be demonstrated. It is the responsibility of the parent to instill values in their children through the use of prayer, reading Bible passages and explaining the limitations of personal freedom. Children need to be nurtured and feel they have a safe haven in their parental relationship. The child does not need to be the recipient of yelling and screaming, often accompanied with profanity. When the parent has a bad day, it should not be taken out on the child. This type of behavior tears down the child's self-esteem. Instead, parents should embrace their children when they cry and console them when they hurt. Children need to be taught that life contains both positive and negative elements.

When parents do not spend quality time with their children, certain questions do not get asked or answered. For example, "How are you doing?" The parent should actively listen to the response to the question. "What have you been up to this week?" Parents should pay special attention to any interactions with other children or adults whom the child mentions. If the child's conversations are snappy and rude it might be a signal that something is wrong and your child needs assistance. Ignoring the situation is a contributor to the problem rather than a proper solution. Silent communication is No Communication! Too often parents respond with, "Whatever!" "Leave me alone!" or "I just cannot wait until you become an adult and get out of my life". As a parent you have the obligation to develop a healthy environment for your child. You must prepare your child to avoid the pitfalls of life such as indulging in drugs, alcohol, illicit sexual conduct, or destructive life-styles. These actions create a confused and underdeveloped person. Whether or not your child becomes a productive member of society is largely due to how well you educate and prepare them.

Active involvement in your child's life lets them know you care about them. As parents we must teach our children to have patience because there are no instant solutions. Your child needs to know that you are not afraid to be an active participant in helping them solve their problems. Positive parental participation can serve as an effective deterrent to negative influences received from movies, videos, "Stars" (Hollywood personalities and sports figures), and peers. Remember, your child's welfare is not something to be left to school teachers, ministers, or other family members. Rearing, loving, and nurturing your child is "Your Holy Responsibility" says God! The Bible says:

Train up a child in the way he should go:
and when he is old, he will not depart from it.
Proverbs 22:6

For the Lord giveth wisdom: out of his mouth
cometh knowledge and understanding.
Proverbs 2:6

When my father and mother forsake me,
then the Lord will take me up.
Psalm 27:20 (KJV)

I will hit this ball so hard that it will find you, Dad, wherever you are.

chapter five

Teenagers Ashley and Charlie Chat — Go Deep, Real Deep

(Parental discretion recommended)

Ashley and Charlie were on the phone for over two hours discussing why their fathers abondoned them. However, their friends are having the same problems with fathers who abondoned them. Ashley told Charlie, "I have a lot of anger inside me. My father always lets me down. I feel confused and angry. Lack of my father's love affected my performance in the 8th and 9th grades. I had trouble getting along with my peers and the teachers. Charlie, do you feel you were being let down by your dad?"

Charlie said, "When I was in middle school, I stayed in the counselor's office quite often. The counselor asked me how I really felt, I told him I was unhappy. I told him I could not think straight. I was miserable and never had anything good to say about my life. The counselor asked me when was the last time I was happy? I would write these words on a piece of paper: NEVER, NEVER, NEVER! This would relieve my frustrations. I would be in a rage because my father did not come to see me. My mother had other children to worry about. The counselor thought I was just being selfish."

"My mother really did not understand that I craved for my father. When I went to school other children and I would cling to the male teachers at our school. We did not have fathers at home and needed their attention. Any given day I would stand with pain and anger in my heart, asking these male teachers for help with my schoolwork. They thought of me as a troubled student. I was trying to ask for help but I did not know how."

Charlie continued, "The littlest thing would upset me. I would be ready to fight someone. I would throw spitballs at other students and call them names. I was miserable. My mother would come up to the school and talk about me in front of the other students. On one occasion I got suspended from school for three days for fighting. As we were leaving school, Mom slapped me. This did not do any good! I would go to my room and play every type of rap music I could, imagining I was a Rapper."

Ashley and Charlie on the phone

"Then I would call my friend, Derrick, and complain about my life to him. Derrick understood me because his father left him when he was five years old. One day Derrick came home from school and his father played with him. He read him a bedtime story, kissed him then said good night. Next, Derrick heard his mother and father arguing. That was the last time he saw his father. Derrick became a problem child for the next five years. He even tried to commit suicide. His mother had to get some counseling for him. Next, she sent him to a different school. Then she started making him participate in after school activities. He was on the debate, chess, swimming and hockey teams. Also, after school Derrick tutored neighborhood children in mathematics. In his spare time he loved to read. Now Derrick is talking about becoming a doctor. Derrick sings baritone at the church he attends. I admire him because he learned to overcome his obstacles."

"My other friend, Beverly, was not as fortunate. Her mother was always drunk," Charlie explained. "Beverly is starved for love. Maybe it has become a cycle because Beverly's mother also never had a father. She made the same mistake her mother made. She had children by men who did not love or care about her. You know Ashley, Beverly's mother put her men before her children. Beverly's mother had babies by different men who always left her. She had no education and was on welfare. She neglected Beverly and her brother, Kevin. Kevin was older than Beverly and stayed in trouble. Their mother would say to them, "All of you are just like your father." She never had any real conversation with them. She was full of self-pity and in denial of her daughter and son's behavior. She blamed everyone but herself. She never tried to correct the problem. When there was noise from arguments at their home, neighbors would just call Protective Services. Kevin was sent to boot camp and it did not help him. Now Kevin and Beverly are in a home for juveniles."

"Beverly was so unhappy with her life that she would come to school ready to fight the other students. Sometimes people blame God for their misery without understanding that we make our own decisions. You know, Ashley, Beverly's father abandoned them when they were born. Their mother should have done more for Beverly and Kevin instead of turning up the bottle. Beverly's mother could have been a successful parent if she had taken the time to bond with her children. She should have given them love and more time. Their mother could have walked them to school or taken them to the market. She did not give them hugs and kisses. The family should have talked it out! In the end, she did not want to change. Ashley, people have to want to change."

Ashley explained that she knew someone who grew up in hell. Ashley commented, "My best friend, Sarah, was abandoned by her mother. She was a heroin addict and a hooker. Sarah was hardly at school to learn anything because she was back and forth at Protective Services. When she did go to school, other kids would make her life a nightmare because they would make fun of her. Sarah had poor hygiene and did not know how to dress. Her hair needed to be combed. All through grade school, Sarah never learned anything and stayed upset. She was disappointed for not knowing her real father. Sarah's mother gave birth to her after having a one-night stand with someone she did not know. She did it in order to pay for drugs. All of Sarah's sisters and brothers have different fathers."

Charlie said, "My mother is a crack addict. I must stop being in denial. First, I must not worry about what others say about my mother and father. Next, I will not compare myself with others and will choose for myself what road I will follow. Finally, I will drop my buddies if they are leading me to prison."

"When I was eleven, I could not read or write. I have found out what I am good at. I am taking up a trade to become an electrician. Maybe I will be an electrical engineer. Each one of us has a gift or talent that we can give to society." "Hey, listen to this poem I wrote":

> Love me
> Watch me grow
> There is no tether,
> No jail, no crime
> That can keep me
> From doing what is wrong.
> It is my own free will."

Ashley told Charlie, "I have a friend named Rachel. Her mother has a top executive job. Rachel's mother gave her everything except love. After Rachel's father left her mother neglected her. She became a workaholic. Now Rachel is depressed and withdrawn. Her mother does not want to deal with Rachel or give her the extra time and love that she requires."

Ashley continued, "My father was a liar. I started hating him because he never wanted to spend time with me. Charlie, no one likes to be lied to. I see why kids today do not respect adults. If someone you love lies to you it causes you to lose trust. We look for leadership in our parents because they are the first people we interact with. These are the closest people we know. They nurture us. My father had a very nice place. He had extra bedrooms. There was no excuse why I could not spend the night with him."

"I would get mad when I thought about how he treated me. When I was about five or six, we went to the movies. Instead of going out to eat after the movie, he would always say he had somewhere to go. He would drop me right back at home immediately after the movie was over. My mother would come outside and become angry because my father did not want to spend any more time with me. Guess what, Charlie. He never bought me anything unless it was my birthday or Christmas. When I turned eleven he stopped bringing me gifts altogether. Charlie, how was the relationship with your father?"

Charlie replied, "Well at least your father came around sometimes. According to some relatives, my father is in prison. Some people tell me my mother had me by a married man. I do not know who my real father is. I get upset at times. I try to hide it. When I am around my friends, I create a father. I make them think he is somebody important. I guess I am really trying to be cool with my friends. I feel ashamed because I do not know my real father. Yet I do know he does not want to be a part of my life. You know, Ashley, it does not make sense that a biological father would turn his back on his own flesh and blood."

Charlie said, "I remember Ashley there were two girls who went to my school and had the same father. The girls both lived around the corner from each other and did not know who their real father was until they passed each other in the hallway and saw that both of them looked alike. Their mother told them later who their father was. I wonder Ashley, how can someone have children everywhere and just do not care about their offspring. It is like me asking my real father why he still could not own up to his child if I was by a married man. He created me with my mother. What's up with that? You know Ashley these unidentified fathers need to start owning up to their unidentified children. I think about it at times."

"I become bitter at times and want to go and hit my father. I have learned to let bygones be bygones," Charlie continued. "You know, Ashley, I started running with the wrong people for the wrong reasons. I was trying to find myself and just wanted to belong to a group. I was looking for love and approval from my friends who are now in jail or dead. I guess that is what turned my life around. My mother was always nagging me about something."

"I used to enjoy marijuana and calling girls out of their names. I tried to impress the girls by wearing designer clothes like the ones you see in magazines. I loved flashing the money that I earned and they had to be older girls or I would not talk to them. I used to love borrowing my friend's car to go to the Mall and pick up older girls. I did not have a driver's license. I wanted a lot of different girls. I wanted to be loved and accepted by them."

"My older sister, Carmen, had the same problem with men. She messed up her life. She was always seeking approval from older men. Carmen believed every man loved her. She was desperate for love. Currently Carmen is an alcoholic and has three children. My mother put her out because they did not get along. My sister really needed my father. He could have taught her how to love herself and develop self esteem."

"Ashley, what really turned my life around was when I saw that the rappers I imitated did not care anything about me. The rappers never come into my neighborhood. On the other hand, my Aunt Patricia always had a kind word for me. I believe she loves me. My Aunt Patricia is genuine. Good people come few and far between. I notice how she treats people. She treats everyone special. You know, Ashley, material things in life cannot make you happy. I felt empty on the inside because I did not have a father."

Ashley said, "Did you know my mother does not trust me? I have not been the perfect person in my mother's eyes since I lied to her. I invited boys over when my mother was not at home. Even when my mother said I could not have company. I did what I wanted to do because she was not at home. When my mother arrived home, she would see me sleeping. I thought, I was making a fool out of her until I got caught, Charlie. I stood boldly in her face telling one lie after another. Now my mother calls me every hour to check on me while she is at work. The phone calls are so frequent that I do not want to pick up the phone. I always check the caller ID."

"My mother put me out several times. Because my attitude toward my mother was, I did not want to do anything for school and work. Also, I felt I was not being loved. If you go to live with your friends, they are only nice for a day. Then they want to know when you are leaving. If you go over to your relative's house, they also want to know when you are leaving. It is horrible when you have to depend on others. Charlie, I learned there is no place like home. I had to do a personality check. I had to examine myself to discover if I was the problem."

"When I went back home, the phone became my best friend. I would call and talk to boys. You can have a lot of guys calling you, Charlie, but many of them just want to talk about going to bed or doing drugs. The guys today like name calling. They call girls "female dogs." I am sure you know what I mean. Most of the girls just want a decent guy. Most of these guys are listening to rap music. They think that they can use the lyrics of the songs to describe girls. The lyrics used are very disrespectful."

"I guess I am starved for attention from a father. In the eighth and ninth grade, I was trying to find myself. I really needed my father but he was not there for me. You see, Charlie, there are others out there who feel the same way we do."

Charlie replied, "Guys about fourteen or fifteen years old look at girls just for sex. They think it is normal. They think it is cool. All the girls think about on the other hand is living for the weekend and going to the Mall. They get their hair and nails done and think they are fabulous. They do not have any conversation besides discussing their hair, nails and clothes."

Ashley says, "Let us talk about going on a date with you guys. It is not a picnic! It is very difficult because the average boy cannot hold a real conversation. Most of the time he is staring at the girl from head to toe. He stares at every girl that walks by. All he talks about is sports, music and clothes. He will ask the girl why she is not smoking pot. It is sad! Why do females have to carry the conversation? I guess a lot of guys have not been exposed to other activities besides sports. They really do not go to plays, science museums, chess tournaments or travel to different places. All they want to do is go to the movies, sit in the back and rub on us girls."

"When a father is an active participant in our lives, he is the role model. He should help us to become adults. He should be helping us to discover our strong points and work toward improving our weaknesses. He should be encouraging us. He should attend Parent-Teacher Conferences and help us with our homework. At the restaurant or on the way to the restaurant, he should listen to what happened to us during the day. There should be interaction!"

Ashley continues, "A lot of girls want approval because they do not have a real father in the home. They look to their mother's boyfriend for approval. They often look to this man for love as well. You often have mothers and daughters competing for attention from the same man. The daughters are trying to establish a relationship with the older man because they did not receive love from their real father."

"Many of the mother's boyfriends take advantage of us girls. They take the mother's money and drive the mother's car. Sometimes they take them to work and ride all day with their friends and other women in her car. For that reason you have to ask your friends to pick you up in order to get home. Friends think you are stupid when they learn that your Mom's boyfriend has the car and does not bring it back until late in the evening."

"You lose your virginity and get put down by friends who still have theirs. If you keep your virginity you get put down by friends who have lost theirs. You see yourself searching, trying to find love. You believe the lies some young boy whispers in your ears. Then one baby after another comes. You lose your way. You make nothing of your life. Next, you become jealous of those who have done well in life. Lack of the biological father in the home has impacted your life and caused you to be your own worst enemy."

"Mentors and role models that you see once a week are not enough," commented Ashley. "They do not see you every day catching hell from peer pressure. They need to be around more often. They do not see us wrestling with fears, frustrations and the misery of not being loved by our fathers."

Charlie says, "If I had a father in the home I would have received the affection that I really needed. Now I guess it is never too late. I am working through my problems. Some children have both parents in the home and their life is still a mess."

Ashley replies, "I have learned how to communicate with others. I have developed a relationship with my mother. I have a job where I interact with people. I desire to become an accountant. I am keeping my life straight. We have both grown up without a real father and it was not easy."

Ashley continues, "My grandmother was my pillar of strength that allowed me to let go of my anger toward my real daddy. My grandmother always wanted me to be happy and go on with my life. She always said, "Life does go on without your daddy". Her love was felt and she gave clothes and food to those in need. I always wondered why she helped others when some folks in the neighborhood did not like her. My grandmother always took me in her arms and gave me hugs and kisses. Her love was genuinely felt. My grandmother is a celebrity who is not featured on radio, television or movie screens. When I think of my grandmother having no legs, confined to a wheelchair, I marvel at the fact that she does not complain about her lack of mobility. My grandmother always tries to uplift other folks by pointing out the good in life. I talked to my grandmother about my situation without a daddy. I asked her questions like why he did not spend time with me. My grandmother's answer to me was, "There are genuine daddys out there who care and there are counterfeit daddys who really just do not care about anything." Also, my grandmother always says, "Put your trust in God. If we obey His word, He will become our light to guide us!"

Charlie replied, "I absolutely agree. In our lives we have had relatives and friends to help us through the rough times. There were teachers and counselors who helped raise our expectations. Our minister has always had a sympathetic ear and wanted us to lead productive lives."

Charlie continued, "Yes, if we think about it there have always been angels surrounding us. I think our folks call them unseen agents for good (chuckle), people like that helpful librarian or that coach who said, "Play fairly by the rules and do not forget to get good grades." Remember that Sunday School teacher who made sure we learned those Bible verses. God has been to both of us, our mother and father. God sends us hugs and kisses even when our earthly parents forget or forsake us. **We do have a Father!"**

Therefore, we, Ashley and Charlie, want to touch other children like ourselves who have no daddy. We wrote these poems titled, "Teach The Children How to Live" and "Lift Yourself Up."

Teach The Children How To Live

We need to teach our children how to live.
Do not let them go astray. Give them hope and dreams.
Teach them how to make their dreams a reality.
Do not let them down. Give them support to make right decisions.

If by chance they go astray, we must keep praying for them.
If they choose the wrong path, positively influence them.
Keep talking to them and encouraging them.
Do not let them down. Give them support to make right decisions.

So we must teach our boys and girls to stop fighting in the streets.
Stop selling drugs. Get a honest job.
Do not let them down. Give them support to make right decisions.

There will be no more dying in the street. No more being shot.
We must teach them how to be responsible.
We must teach them how to make right decisions.

Sometimes say no! Do not always say yes. It will help in the end.
Everything should not go their way.
Do not let them down. Give them support to make right decisions.

Teach the children to not expect everyone to care.
Everyone will not be willing to help them.
Do not get mad. Just keep moving forward.
Do not let them down. Give them support to make right decisions.

References

Crisfield, Deborah. Dysfunctional Families. New York: Crestwood House, 1992, pp. 26-27, 39-40

Copelnd, Peter and Hamer, Dean. Living With Our Genes. Why They Matter More Than You Think. New York: Dell Publishing Group Inc, March 1998, pp. 6-7, 12

Davis, Laura. I Thought We'd Never Speak Again. New York: Harper Collins Publishers, 2002, pp 106-107, 245

Dortch, Thomas W. Jr. Miracles of Mentoring. Broadway New York: Doubleday, a Division of Random House, Inc., 2000, pp. 87-91

Keyes, Ken Jr. and Keyes, Penny. The Power of Unconditional Love. Coos Bay, Oregon: Love Line, 1990, pp. 68-69, 80-83

Lawson, Ann. Kids and Gangs. Minneapolis: Johnson Institute, 1994, pp. 47-48

Leslie, Charles. Why is Everyone So Cranky? New York: Hyperion, 1999, pp. 24, 289

Mancini, Richard E. Living With A Single Parent. New York: The Rosen Publishing Group, Inc., 1992, pp. 11, 21, 53

To Be Continued...

ASHLEY AND CHARLIE